WAITING ON GOD
From Sorrow to Submission
A 21-Day Devotional

Renate McDonald

Copyright © 2023 Renaté McDonald

All rights reserved. No part of this publication may be reproduced or transmitted in any form or by any means, electronic or mechanical, including photocopy, recording or any information storage and retrieval system without permission in writing from the publisher and author.

ISBN: 978-1-958443-48-4 (paperback)

Unless otherwise noted, all scriptures are from THE HOLY BIBLE, ENGLISH STANDARD VERSION®, Copyright© 2001 by Crossway, a publishing ministry of Good News Publishers. Used by permission. All rights reserved.

Scripture quotations marked (AMPC) are taken from the Amplified® Bible (AMPC), Copyright © 1954, 1958, 1962, 1964, 1965, 1987 by The Lockman Foundation. Used by permission. All rights reserved.

Scripture quotations marked (NASB) are taken from the NEW AMERICAN STANDARD BIBLE®, Copyright© 1960, 1962, 1963, 1968, 1971, 1972, 1973, 1975, 1977, 1995 by The Lockman Foundation. Used by permission. All rights reserved.

Scripture quotations marked (AMP) are taken from the AMPLIFIED® BIBLE, Copyright© 1954, 1958, 1962, 1964, 1965, 1987 by the Lockman Foundation. Used by permission. All rights reserved.

Scripture quotations marked (NIV) are taken from THE HOLY BIBLE, NEW INTERNATIONAL VERSION®. Copyright© 1973, 1978, 1984, 2011 by Biblica, Inc.™. Used by permission. All rights reserved.

Scripture quotations marked (TPT) are from The Passion Translation®. Copyright © 2017, 2018, 2020 by Passion & Fire Ministries, Inc. Used by permission. All rights reserved. ThePassionTranslation.com.

A catalogue record for this book is available from the National Library of Jamaica.

Cover design by: Shavel Grayson

Published by:

DAYELight
PUBLISHERS

DayeLight Publishers
www.dayelightpublishers.com

Dedication

To my husband, Jermaine McDonald, who has been God's mouthpiece to me throughout this process of waiting. You are my biggest supporter and steadfast prayer partner.

To our Jellybean, my constant reminder to see the joy in life regardless of the circumstances.

- AND -

To my mother, Christine Walker, who has shown me daily what it means to wait with grace.

I thank God for you all.

Acknowledgements

Without God, I can do nothing. He must therefore get the first mention and all the praise! I am humbled to have been chosen as the vessel for the writing of this book. As long as it took and as daunting as it felt, each step of the way, I knew God was with me. So, thank You, Father, for pouring into me that I may pour into others.

To my husband, Jermaine, who believed in me more than I believed in myself at times - thank you. Thank you for the encouraging words and your understanding stance when I stayed up late to write or study the Word. Thank you for praying over me when things got overwhelming. Thank you for being there through it all and remaining my number one fan.

To my family and friends who are always cheering me on to do what the Lord sends me to do – thank you. Your love and support are priceless.

To my amazing editors – Tasharae Nicholson and Chaday Nelson – who did not skip a beat when I asked for help. You are phenomenal. Thank you for sharing your time and your feedback. Your affirmations helped to bring this book to life.

To my Pastors who have impacted my life more than I can say – thank you. Founding Pastors Dwight and Joan Fletcher, Pastors Jean-Claude and Marsha Davidson, Pastors Paul and Andrea Russell and Pastor Maurice, each of you has poured into me and built me up in my walk with the Lord and I thank you.

To my church family, especially my mentors – Auntie Ivy "Esther" Bradshaw, Aldith Hazzart and Deborah Johnson - you ladies have changed my life in such significant ways in different seasons of my life and you continue to be safe havens for me. Thank you.

To my mentees who allowed me to share some of this

body of work to help you through your own challenges, thank you. Your openness and honesty about your own journeys helped me to see even clearer the need for this book.

To my fellow person in waiting, yes, you, the one reading this, thank you! Thank you for taking the time to read the devotional and process through your pain.

Table of Contents

Dedication ii
Acknowledgements iv
Introduction viii
ACKNOWLEDGE THE PAIN 11
   Share Your Feelings with God 12
   The Pain of Waiting 16
   Commit Yourself to the Lord 19
   The Power of Community 23
UNDERSTAND THE PAIN 27
   Seek God's Perspective 28
   Seek Wisdom; Do Not Be Swayed 31
   You Will Not Be Put To Shame 34
   Endurance 37
SURRENDER THE PAIN 41
   Wait With Expectation 42
   God's Will Prevails 45
   Your Identity is in Christ 49
   Worship While You Wait 53
   God's Timing is Perfect 57
RESTORE HOPE 61
   Wait on the Lord and be Renewed 62
   Bring Forth Fruit in its Season 65
   God is Still Faithful 69
   Remain Confident in God 73
SUBMIT COMPLETELY 77

Make Room for Your Promise 78
Say Goodbye to Doubt.. 82
Hold Firm to God's Promises 86
Wait Well 90

Introduction

"Obedience is better than sacrifice..."

1 Samuel 15:22 ESV

This verse has stuck with me since I learned it a few years ago, and that is what has led to the writing of this devotional - obedience.

In the early stages of my walk with the Lord, there was nothing I wanted more than to conceive a child with my husband. My prayers were mainly focused on that one desire and every month I dealt with painful sorrow. Through it all, I continued to read the Bible, pray regularly, go to church, and everything else to grow in relationship with God.

One day I realized that my prayers were shifting. I wanted to genuinely know God more. I sought after Him. I started pouring myself into serving Him and being obedient to His leading. I still wanted a child, and the desire would explode in me from time to time resulting in many tears, questions, doubts, fears, and everything in between. This continued for a few years.

One day in September 2020, I broke. I was a leader in my church, I had an active relationship with the Lord, and I was thriving in other areas of my life, but on that day, I was faced with a truth I didn't want to see – I was hiding a piece of my heart from the Lord out of fear of being hurt by Him.

I had been disappointed many times before so I began to build a wall around this part of my heart so God wouldn't touch it.

This realization floored me, and I cried out to God pained that I had tried to lock Him out and exhausted from trying to keep it together on my own. I cried myself to sleep that night, with occasional utterances to the Lord about what I was feeling. But the next morning, I felt like a new creation. There was something powerful in that breaking, that repenting, that vulnerability before Him that made room for rebirth and full submission to His will.

As God continues to work in me, He has chosen to work through me with this devotional.

The lessons I have learned over the last eleven years of walking through my wait have been packaged in this 21-day devotional to help you to wait well, regardless of what you are waiting for. The waiting season can feel unending but sometimes, it's a matter of perspective.

What if you shifted your attitude from waiting with entitlement to waiting with a heart of service (as a great waiter at a restaurant would wait on you)? How different would your experience be if your questions became:

- How can I serve You today, Lord?
- What would You have me do for You today, Lord?

How would your life look if you actively sought first the Kingdom of God daily?

This devotional is written to help you do exactly that. It is written through the lens of my experiences and teachings that I have received from the Holy Spirit, reinforced by the unchanging Word of God.

The book is organized in five sections to help you:

1. Acknowledge the pain
2. Understand the pain 3. Surrender the pain
3. Restore hope
4. Submit completely

Each day is accompanied by:

- A journaling prompt
- A prayer prompt
- A journaling page

They are meant to get you started in your reflections and conversations with God to get to the core of what He wants to address in that area of your life. Take the time you need to process through each day and journal whatever comes to the surface for you.

I pray that as you work through each day, you will open yourself up to receive the healing that the Lord has for you. May you go from sorrow to submission, in Jesus' name. Amen.

Your Waiting Partner,
Ren

Share Your Feelings with God

"I am weary with my moaning; every night I flood my bed with tears; I drench my couch with my weeping."

Psalm 6:6 ESV

At first thought, you may say to yourself, "Why do I need to say what I am feeling to God when He already knows all?" While God truly knows all, He wants you to open your mouth and heart to Him for your own benefit. When you are willing to communicate your feelings with God, you are letting Him into those areas you previously tried to keep to yourself; those areas you felt were too painful to discuss, even with God.

As you are in your season of waiting for what the Lord has for you, think on your life:

- Are you trying to protect yourself from disappointment by not talking about it?
- Are you keeping your true feelings buried so that you don't have to deal with the pain, or better yet, the growth that is needed to handle that gift you are waiting for?

Sometimes, you can convince yourself that not talking about it is the best thing to do but when you do that, you are hindering the transformative work that God intends to do in your life.

Emotions are not innately bad, instead, they are meant to be indicators. For example, fear indicates danger, while joy indicates fulfilment and satisfaction. If you bury your feelings, then you are also burying the opportunity to identify what needs to be adjusted in your life. So, instead of burying them, how about exploring them with God, allowing Him to bring forth fresh revelation about what you are experiencing?

When we read the Psalms, we see numerous examples of David – a man after God's own heart – pouring out his worries, pains, joy, fears, all his emotions to the Lord. In Psalm 6:6, David shares his weary heart with God, lamenting his nightly crying. He is worn out and frustrated but still trusting God enough to be open and honest with his emotions. Likewise, you can go before the Lord, trusting Him with your heart – He will bottle your tears (see Psalm 56:8) and deliver you.

Understand this, over the time that your pain has been buried or un-surrendered, you would have likely built up some walls or habits that need to be broken all the way down and stripped away from you. Your brokenness and vulnerability before the Lord are required to allow Him to rebuild you in His intended way. He puts your broken pieces together in a beautiful mosaic, truly using all your experiences, mistakes, and all for the good of those who love God and are called according to His purpose (see Romans 8:28). Your healing begins when you let Him in. The initial pain of being broken in the presence of God can be very hard but the result of that surrender is priceless freedom.

Journaling Prompt:
Will you make the decision to be vulnerable with God today, verbalizing to Him the pain you have held on to?

Take note of your thoughts and feelings about this. Write down the areas that you are acknowledging as painful.

Prayer Prompt:
Dear Lord, I thank You for being my ever-present help in my times of need. Today, Lord, I need You desperately to help me to trust You with all my heart and my deepest emotions. Help me to believe that You will take care of my brokenness. This process may not come easily for me, so I pray for more grace as I come to You today to confess my true emotions to You. Forgive me for not trusting You before Lord and please help me to lay it all before You now, in Jesus' name I pray. Amen.

[Continue this prayer as you are led by sharing the emotions you have held on to with God. Trust that He will bring revelation where needed.]

> *"You have taken account of my wanderings; Put my tears in Your bottle.*
> *Are they not in Your book?"*
>
> Psalm 56:8 NASB1995

Let's Journal ... Waiting on GOD:

From Sorrow to Submission

The Pain of Waiting

"So it went on year by year. As often as she went up to the house of the Lord, she [Peninah] used to provoke her [Hannah]. Therefore Hannah wept and would not eat."

1 Samuel 1:7 ESV

Waiting on a move of God can be painful (see Proverbs 13:12). When the desires of your heart are not yet fulfilled, you may be tempted to think that there is something you have or have not done to deserve what feels like punishment. In 1 Samuel 1, we see that Hannah had no children (her womb was closed), and this fuelled much provocation from Peninnah. Hannah worshipped year after year, believing that her blessing and relief would come but as she waited, it probably felt like her breakthrough was taking a lifetime to come.

Did this mean that Hannah had displeased God or that she was being punished by Him? There is nothing in the text to lead us to believe that. The wait was a part of her preparation. It was preparing her to mother a child who would become a powerful man of God. It was preparing her to handle the challenges that would come later in her life as she gave her child, Samuel, back to the Lord. (Just think what it would be like to give up the child for whom you travailed in prayer). The wait was building her character and her faith in God. She eventually poured her heart out to God, promising to return to Him the child she so desperately wanted to birth (see 1 Samuel 1:9-18). She was now willing to sacrifice her heart's desire for God's greater purpose.

I encourage you today to surrender your pain to God just as Hannah did and place your trust in Him for what He has planned for your life. Lean into the process and preparation you are now going through, and trust that it will help you in the coming seasons.

Journaling Prompt:
Whatever you are waiting for in this season of your life, however painful it may feel to you right now, ask yourself this:

- "Do I believe that God has a plan for me that demonstrates His unmatched love for me?"
- "Am I willing to say "yes" to God's plan even if it looks like I will not get what I want?"

Take note of any other emotions or thoughts that have been stirred in you as you went through this time of devotion today.

Prayer Prompt:
Lord, the pain of this wait is heavy. I do not want to carry it anymore. Today, I release it all to You – every heartache, every disappointment, every tear. I trust in You and Your plan for me. Help me to come into alignment with You, embracing this process and all You have for me, in Jesus' name. Amen.

Let's Journal ... Waiting on GOD:

From Sorrow to Submission

Commit Yourself to the Lord

"...I and my young women will also fast as you do. Then I will go to the king, though it is against the law, and if I perish, I perish."

Esther 4:16b ESV

When you share your feelings with God, you can be tempted to wallow in self-pity or to ask the infamous question, "Why me?" Over time, as my relationship with the Lord grew, I have learned to truly embrace that we each have a path to walk, a journey to embark on, a role to play in the body of Christ...and each one is important. Your wait may feel burdensome but always remember these three things:

- Jesus has promised to be with you to the end of the age (see Matthew 28:20) – You are not alone; come into alignment with Him. "God's grace is sufficient for you, for power is perfected in weakness" (see 2 Corinthians 12:9) – Trust His plan.
- You work from a place of rest when you are yoked (tethered) to Jesus (see Matthew 11:28-30) – Stay connected to Him.

Waiting is an action word. It requires intentional thought and execution; otherwise, you will be tossed by every wave and become an emotional "wave-rider." Every thought that comes, whether positive or negative, carries you on an emotional wave and you simply ride it until it is over.

The truth is the enemy loves when believers take that passive approach to waiting. Why? Because it makes it easier for him to influence our thoughts, actions, and beliefs.

If you look at the book of Esther, you will see that Queen Esther was in a predicament – there was a plan to murder her people (the Jews), but her uncle, Mordecai, asked her to intervene. She also knew that if she approached the king without him first requesting her presence, then she would be at risk of being put to death. So, what did she do? She committed herself to the Lord in prayer and fasting as she prepared to approach the king. She sought God's favour because she knew that He was the source of her strength and that He was ultimately in control. As she committed to the fast, she also resolved that she would accept whatever the outcome would be. In Esther 4:16b she says, "…if I perish, I perish." This was a state of full surrender to God's plan, even to the point of death.

Can you say the same of yourself? Are you aligned with God's plan, trusting Him, and staying connected to Him so that you can confidently embrace whatever outcome is on the other side of your waiting period?

If not, then make the decision today to put your life squarely in God's hands and commit your whole self to Him so that you may fulfil your role within the body of Christ.

Journaling Prompt:
Consider the areas in your life where you are out of alignment with God. Ask the Holy Spirit to show you where you have stepped outside of God's plan for your life.

Take note of these areas and actively commit to realign with God's purpose for you.

Prayer Prompt:
Lord, today I confess that I have not committed myself wholly and completely to You. Please forgive me and help me to fully embrace Your plan for my life, even as I wait to see it unfold. My heart is heavy as I wait for my desire for _____ to be fulfilled. I surrender that to You now, Lord, in exchange for Your burden which is light. I commit myself to You on this day, and I pray for Your strength to empower me in my weakness, in Jesus' name. Amen.

"For My yoke is easy and My burden is light."

Matthew 11:30 NASB1995

Let's Journal... Waiting on GOD:

From Sorrow to Submission

The Power of Community

"Two are better than one because they have a good return for their labour. For if either of them falls, the one will lift up his companion. But woe to the one who falls when there is not another to lift him up.
Furthermore, if two lie down together they keep warm, but how can one be warm alone? And if one can overpower him who is alone, two can resist him. A cord of three strands is not quickly torn apart."

Ecclesiastes 4:9-12 NASB1995

One of the greatest challenges we face while waiting on God for anything is the temptation to believe that we're doing it alone.

Oftentimes, that thing you are waiting for is so precious to you that you do not want to share it with anyone. It can become an avenue of isolation, and it can even lead to idolatry as you may begin to treasure the desired gift more than the proven Giver.

But here's the truth – God has placed you in a community of believers because you are not meant to walk your journey alone. While the Lord may take you through seasons of consecration when He is preparing you for a specific assignment (think of Moses, Noah, Jesus), it is not His desire for you to do all your life without meaningful connections.

Your church community is there as a part of God's plan to refine and draw you closer to Himself. This happens through your community serving you and you serving them, and ultimately building healthy relationships. In these relationships, you can share your heart, including that thing which you most desire.

What you are most likely to find is compassion, encouragement, strength, and support.

When you give yourself to community, you will have an opportunity to rest from your toil. Ecclesiastes 4:8 speaks of the endless toil of a man without dependents. The following verse tells us of the good return for labour when there are two instead of just one. In godly community, you will have support to carry your burdens to the Lord, to storm the gates of heaven, and even to rest from your labour because there are others working alongside you who will continue to carry out God's purposes while you rest.

These are the people who you can share your heart with and trust that they will walk with you on the journey, even when it gets tough. Others have a greater ability to empathize with you than you know. Moreover, there are others going through the same struggles and waiting on the same solutions as you. This is an opportunity to connect with others and receive the help you need to carry your burden (of waiting) to the Lord in faith.

A strong godly community can be the difference between you suffering silently with a façade of doing well and you actually living in the freedom that Jesus came to earth, suffered, died, resurrected, and ascended to heaven to provide for you.

God wants you to connect with others and thrive in communities where you fight together against the schemes of the enemy, who seeks to tempt you with lies, loneliness, and isolation.

I challenge you today to take an active approach towards building your godly community, make real connections and share your burden with a trustworthy friend.

Journaling Prompt:
Examine your community of friends today. Ask the Holy Spirit to show you the persons in your life who are there by God's design to help you on your journey. Ask Him to show you who you should trust with your wait.

Prayer Prompt:
Heavenly Father, thank You for providing all that I need to walk this journey. I repent of holding this desire so tightly that I am unable to see what You desire for me now. Help me to see the truth that You have provided Your church as a community among Your people and that Your plans for me are perfect. Help me to find where You want me to be in this season, not just for what I can get but also for what I can give. I release my desires to You, Father. I submit my heart to You, in Jesus' name. Amen.

"And let us consider how we may spur one another on toward love and good deeds, 25 not giving up meeting together..."

Hebrews 10:24-25a NIV

Let's Journal... Waiting on GOD:

From Sorrow to Submission

Seek God's Perspective

"Do not be conformed to this world (this age), [fashioned after and adapted to its external, superficial customs], but be transformed (changed) by the [entire] renewal of your mind [by its new ideals and its new attitude], so that you may prove [for yourselves] what is the good and acceptable and perfect will of God, even the thing which is good and acceptable and perfect [in His sight for you]."

Romans 12:2 AMP

It is easy and very tempting to get caught up in what we see around us and what we are fed by culture because we are physically in this world. Sometimes, without even realizing it, we begin to believe what we are fed by the world over what we are assured of by the Word of God. John 15:19 tells us that we are in the world but not of it. That is, as followers of Christ, God has chosen us out of the world and we therefore should look, think and act differently from the rest of the world. To do that, we must be transformed by the renewing of our minds through the internalizing of the truth of God's Word. This renewal allows us to see ourselves and situations from God's perspective, then to respond accordingly. It allows us to identify His perfect will in every situation and to see past our emotions which are fleeting.

This renewal I speak of is not a one-time event but a continuous process, one that requires our commitment and active participation. You must intentionally and consistently read the Word, spend time in prayer, spend quiet time listening to God's voice and then follow His instructions. It is through these disciplines that you reinforce your connection with God, and you are therefore able to live according to His will.

Today's encouragement: God has the blueprint for your life. Although He may not reveal every detail of it to you all at once, He cares for you and loves you more than you can even imagine. Trust His will and His way above all else.

Journaling Prompt:
What has your thought-life been like? Have you been focused on what the world is dictating or what God has promised? Are you taking in God's Word and actively participating in the process of renewing your mind? As you wait, are you seeking God's perfect will or simply your own?

Prayer Prompt:
Lord, forgive me for the times that I give in to the temptations of this world, thinking and acting as the world dictates instead of standing firm on the truth of Your Word. Today, Lord, I submit myself to You completely, and I pray for the desire to actively participate in the renewal of my mind so that I may prove Your good, acceptable, and perfect will for my life. Help me to see this period of waiting from Your perspective, in Jesus' name I pray. Amen.

"...because you are not of the world, but I chose you out of the world, therefore the world hates you."

John 15:19 ESV

Let's Journal... Waiting on GOD:

From Sorrow to Submission

6

Seek Wisdom; Do Not Be Swayed

"But he must ask [for wisdom] in faith, without doubting [God's willingness to help], for the one who doubts is like a billowing surge of the sea that is blown about and tossed by the wind."

James 1:6 AMP

In this season of waiting, it is particularly important to discern God's perfect will and to live in accordance with that. There are so many distractions and detractors that come our way, whether through the media, well-intentioned friends and family, our internal thoughts, or otherwise. If we are not firmly planted in relationship with God, we can be easily tossed about like the waves of the sea (see James 1:6), and our faith wavers.

As you continue this journey of seeking after God and the renewing of your mind, dig deeper into the Word of God. Search Him out. Pray continuously and in faith. The enemy tries to encourage us to doubt God's Word and to doubt our convictions in Christ because he knows that doubt makes us unstable and less effective against his schemes. Hebrews 6:19 reminds us that we have a hope in Christ, which anchors our soul. This hope is firm and secure. When we remain in Him, although the journey is an emotional one and we may get discouraged along the way, our hope always remains. Why? Because God is not a man that He should lie so if He said it, He will do it (see

Numbers 23:19). Your role is to stand in agreement with what He has said, keep believing, remain steadfast in hope, and stay obedient to God. He will do what He said.

Do not lose hope; do not give in to doubt. God never fails. Remain in His truth. He will do what He said.

Journaling Prompt:
Where has your faith been wavering? Where have you cast doubt on God's Word? Ask God to show you where there may be cracks in the foundation of your faith, then write down the truth from God's Word that counter these doubts.

Prayer Prompt:
Lord, I thank You for Your faithfulness and unconditional love. Forgive me for the times that I have doubted You. Today I commit to being and remaining anchored in You, Jesus. I have no desire to be tossed about like the waves. Give me discernment and wisdom to know when I am going off-course. Provide Your gentle correction, Lord, and let my heart be open to receive it without rebellion. I put my faith and trust in You, Lord. You never fail. May every moment of my waiting journey bring glory and honour to Your name. Use me, Lord, in Jesus' name. Amen.

> *"God is not man, that He should lie,*
> *or a son of man, that He should change his mind.*
> *Has He said, and will He not do it?*
> *Or has He spoken, and will He not fulfil it?"*
>
> Numbers 23:19 ESV

Let's Journal... Waiting on GOD:

From Sorrow to Submission

You Will Not Be Put To Shame

"Do not be afraid; you will not be put to shame. Do not fear disgrace; you will not be humiliated. You will forget the shame of your youth and remember no more the reproach of your widowhood."

Isaiah 54:4 NIV

As we wait, temptations arise to shift our focus from God and towards self. Thoughts of "Why me?" "Why hasn't it happened yet?" "What is so wrong with me that I need ALL this refining before seeing the promise?" "Lord, have You forgotten me?" and more can start to creep in.

Feelings of fear lurk nearby, tempting you to believe that you are getting too old for the promise to still be possible. You may entertain feelings of shame. You may even begin to feel foolish for having believed this promise in the first place. Today, God is saying to you, "Stop!" Repent of that wrong thinking, turn away from unbelief, shame, and fear. You will not be put to shame. His Word will not fall to the ground. Take comfort in His Word that you will not be humiliated. Even more than that, God is not a man that He should lie. If He said it, He will do it.

Hold tight to the promises that He has spoken over your life. His promises are not to be confused with our earthly desires though. Continue seeking after God and His will so that you will be holding on to the right thing in each season.

In *1 John 5:14-15*, the Word of God says,

"This is the confidence we have in approaching God: that if we ask anything according to His will, He hears us. And if we know that He hears us—whatever we ask—we know that we have what we asked of Him." (NIV)

It is in seeking and knowing His will that we can confidently approach God, knowing that we will not be put to shame.

Today's encouragement: Seek God's promises for your life. Take hold of them. Rest in knowing that He will not allow you, His child and treasure, to be put to shame.

Journaling Prompt:
Take some time today to write down any fears, doubts, shame, and wrong beliefs you may be carrying as it pertains to God's promises to you. Ask Holy Spirit to reveal your own heart to you in this area and to show You Scriptures that reinforce truth.

Prayer Prompt:
Lord, I thank You that Your Word is true, and I can depend on You always. Please forgive me for harbouring these wrong beliefs, doubts, fears, and shame [call by name each one you wrote down]. I surrender them all to You, and I break agreement with these thoughts and beliefs now in Jesus' name. Help me to stand firm on Your Word, knowing that You will not put me to shame. I thank You for Your faithfulness and Your peace over my life in Jesus' name. Amen.

Let's Journal... Waiting on GOD:

From Sorrow to Submission

Endurance

"Consider it nothing but joy, my brothers and sisters, whenever you fall into various trials. Be assured that the testing of your faith [through experience] produces endurance [leading to spiritual maturity, and inner peace]. And let endurance have its perfect result and do a thorough work, so that you may be perfect and completely developed [in your faith], lacking in nothing."

James 1:2-4 AMP

The challenges we face in life are many, but each one has a purpose. James reminds us to "count it nothing but joy" when we face these challenges because they test our faith, which builds endurance. During your wait, the trials may look like periods of doubt, ridicule from others, temptations to go with what the world says, loneliness, feelings of rejection, or several other challenges.

For my husband and me, they have looked like:

- Doubts about our ability to be good parents.
- Facing ridicule and judgment for not proceeding with assisted fertility treatment because God said it was not for us at that time.
- Temptations to disobey God's instructions regarding In-Vitro Fertilization (IVF).
- Feeling incomplete and lonely.
- Feeling as if God has forgotten about us and we're getting too old to see the fulfilment of His promise.

- Battling with executing God's instructions to us out of fear of still not seeing the promise.
- Questioning our worthiness of receiving His promises.

We have been through all that and more, but what has come out of it all? We have learned what it means to endure - never letting go of the truth of God's Word and His character, and remaining hopeful and prayerful. Although the emotions can be difficult, our faith is anchored in Jesus Christ and His finished work on the cross, which firmly established His Sovereignty over all things.

When you do not see the promise and you continue praying, you continue believing, there is a transformation happening in your spirit. You are learning how to lean on God and how to live for Him and not just for yourself.

Think about it – why is seeing this promise so important to you? Are you at a place where you can honestly say that your desire for the promise is mainly for God's glory and secondarily for your fulfilment? Do not get me wrong, God does want you to enjoy the life He has given you, but His mandate to us all is to "Seek **first** the Kingdom of God and **His** righteousness…" *(see Matthew 6:33, emphasis mine)* and then "all these things will be added unto you." God must come first in your life.

For this to happen, you need endurance to keep believing and to keep trusting when things get challenging. You need strengthened faith to continue proclaiming the promises of God though they are yet to be seen. Amidst it all, you can remain joyful because you know that His promises are "Yes" and "Amen." Embrace the challenges as they strengthen you for what else is to come.

I believe this is what James referred to in James 1:2-4.

Journaling Prompt:
Will you choose to endure and allow your faith to be strengthened for the rest of this waiting journey? Take some time to write down the challenge(s) you are currently facing and the maturation that you are experiencing because of it/them.

Prayer Prompt:
Heavenly Father, forgive me for the times I have allowed my emotions to overshadow the work You are seeking to do in me. Give me the determination to endure through the challenges and come out with stronger faith in You. Help me to fix my focus on You and things meant for Your glory over my selfish desires. Examine my heart, Lord, and give me Your loving correction that I may walk rightly with You and in the purpose to which You have called me, in Jesus' precious name I pray. Amen.

> "Count it all joy, my brothers, when you meet trials of various kinds, for you know that the testing of your faith produces steadfastness. And let steadfastness have its full effect, that you may be perfect and complete, lacking in nothing."
>
> James 1:2-4 ESV

Let's Journal ... Waiting on GOD:

From Sorrow to Submission

SURRENDER
THE PAIN

● ● ●

Wait With Expectation

"In the morning, Lord, you hear my voice; in the morning I lay my requests before you and wait expectantly."

Psalm 5:3 NIV

God wants us to remain in expectation of His move. It is often tempting for us to push aside the things that God has told us to wait for. We bury it, stop thinking about it, and stop praying about it out of fear of disappointment. But God has promised never to leave nor forsake us (see Deuteronomy 31:6), and His Word never fails (see Matthew 24:35). In Psalm 5:3, the psalmist says he lays his requests before the Lord and waits expectantly. Even without knowing HOW or WHEN the Lord will move, we can trust that He will do what He has promised to do.

What does waiting expectantly look like? It looks like continued prayer, a hopeful outlook, trusting that God will do what He said He would do. It looks like walking in obedience regarding what the Lord is saying to you during the waiting season, knowing that He is preparing you for the thing you are waiting for.

In this season of waiting, the Lord desires to pour into you, to refine you and prepare you to receive that thing you have been waiting for, all for His glory. Will you let Him?

This will require your obedience, some sacrifice and intentional time spent with the Lord to hear His heart. It may be uncomfortable, but it will be worth it. Press into Him. Be open and vulnerable with Him. He can protect your heart better than you ever would be able to. Trust Him with it. He is for you.

Journaling Prompt:
Ask God to show you where you may have lost hope in His promises. Write it down. Then ask God to show you the path to renewed hope.

Prayer Prompt:
Lord, I thank You that You are always faithful. Forgive me for the times that I have lost hope and have let go of Your promises. Help me to be faithful to You and to hold on to Your promises even when things don't look the way I expect. Help me to continue laying my requests before you with expectancy in my heart. You are my God whose Word never fails. Please help me to be steadfast and expectant in this season of waiting, in Jesus' name I pray. Amen.

"Heaven and earth will pass away, but my words will not pass away."

Matthew 24:35 ESV

Let's Journal ... Waiting on GOD:

From Sorrow to Submission

God's Will Prevails

"So will My word be which goes out of My mouth; It will not return to Me void (useless, without result), Without accomplishing what I desire, and without succeeding in the matter for which I sent it. For you will go out [from exile] with joy and be led forth [by the Lord Himself] with peace; The mountains and the hills will break forth into shouts of joy before you, and all the trees of the field will clap their hands. Instead of the thorn bush the cypress tree will grow, and instead of the nettle the myrtle tree will grow; And it will be a memorial to the Lord, for an everlasting sign [of His mercy] which will not be cut off."

Isaiah 55:11-13 AMP

In this period of preparing to receive your blessing, there may be things that seem irrelevant to the promise. They are not. God is the greatest strategist there is, and He truly works all things together for the good of those who love Him and keep His commands (see Romans 8:28). He wastes nothing.

This became very real to us as we entered our 9th year of waiting to conceive a child. In year 4 of this journey, the Lord impressed on us to purchase a onesie. We did. Then, He told us to give to another couple. It seemed illogical and hurtful to us at the time. We worked through those emotions and moved forward in obedience. We gave it to the couple to whom we were led. Less than six months later, they visited to share that they were pregnant. This, after being told by doctors that natural conception would have been problematic. We love that child so much. That couple eventually told us that they would keep the onesie until they were released to return it to us. We waited every year for its return.

Exactly four years after they visited to share about their pregnancy, we went to see our friends as they were preparing to move to another country. On that day, they returned the onesie in perfect condition. Our hearts were overjoyed. What seemed like a random statement four years before and a natural visit with friends, turned out to be God's way of keeping alive our hope in Him and His promise. Our children are not here yet, but our faith in Christ is alive and active.

In Isaiah 55:11, the Lord says His Word will not return to Him void. It will do what He intends. When our friend said she would not return the onesie until it was time, the Lord spoke through her. We believe that it is indeed time to see our promise come to pass. We wait expectantly for the Lord as we continue to seek His face in every area of our lives. Verse 12 says you will go out in joy and be led by peace. Joy and peace, two fruits of the Holy Spirit, are good indicators of His presence and action in your life. As you follow where He leads, you will see His will prevail. I believe with you today for the fulfilment of God's promise to you.

Journaling Prompt:
Think about the promise/promises you are waiting on. What has God done/shown you to encourage you as you wait? How has He reassured you that His will shall prevail? Write that down as an encourager for times of doubt.

Prayer Prompt:
Oh Lord, increase my faith and hope in You, my King. Let my desire for Your will be so great that I walk willingly where You lead, trusting that Your Word over my life will

come to pass. In Your Word it says that it will not return to You void. Help me, Lord, not to waiver in my belief and hope for Your promise. Help me to truly trust You. Give me revelation that I may see Your hand in even the seemingly mundane things in my life. I pray this in Jesus' name. Amen.

Let's Journal... Waiting on GOD:

> "And we know that for those who love God all things work together for good, for those who are called according to his purpose."
>
> Romans 8:28 ESV

From Sorrow To Submission

Your Identity is in Christ

"For we are His workmanship, created in Christ Jesus for good works, which God prepared beforehand so that we would walk in them."

Ephesians 2:10 ESV

When you are in a season of waiting, it can become very tempting to define yourself by the thing you are waiting for – "a barren woman," "a single woman," "a single man," "a childless man," "a jobless person," and the list goes on. When the temptations come, it is the perfect time to enforce your 2 Corinthians 10:5 authority, taking captive every thought and making them subject to Christ. While these descriptors may be true of your situation, they do not define you. You may be without a child, without a spouse or without a job, etc., but that is not the sum-total of who you are, nor is it the main feature of who you are.

As a follower of Jesus Christ, your identity is in Him. Ephesians 2:10 affirms that we are God's workmanship, created in Christ Jesus. The identity of Christ is imputed unto us as we are born again and come into genuine relationship with Him. We become righteous, holy, and worthy in God's eyes as we continuously seek Him first in all things. This is the identity that you are meant to hold on to. This is the truth that replaces the lies that try to define you by your circumstances.

God knitted you together with intention and a plan. He has

the blueprint of your life. He has held you through all your life's experiences, allowing you to become who you are today for a reason. He has good work for you to do – work that He has prepared beforehand (see Ephesians 2:10). So instead of looking at your circumstance as a label to negatively define you, how about shifting your perspective by asking your heavenly Father what He intends for you to do with this current reality? How can this situation be used for His glory instead of your distress?

By embracing the truth of your identity in Christ and dismissing the lie of your identity being in your circumstance, you are opening yourself up to hearing clearly from God where He wants you to go.

Journaling Prompt:
Are you willing to be a living sacrifice unto God, choosing His plan over your own, believing that His plan is for the ultimate good? A good test of this is to ask yourself, "If I do not receive that thing I am waiting for, what will my response to God be?" If you can honestly answer that question affirming that you will still love and serve God with all that you are, then you know that you believe Him and trust His Sovereignty. If you are not there yet, then ask God to help your unbelief in this.

Prayer Prompt:
Lord, I thank You that You thought of me and crafted me so intentionally in Christ. I repent of believing the lies about who I am. Today, I shed every wrong belief about my identity, and I hold firm to who You say I am and who You have made me to be. Open my eyes to Your truth. Help me to see beyond my feelings and my situation, and to choose You above all else every day. I surrender to You, Lord, in Jesus' name. Amen.

"We destroy arguments and every lofty opinion raised against the knowledge of God, and take every thought captive to obey Christ."

2 Corinthians 10:5 ESV

Let's Journal... Waiting on GOD:

From Sorrow to Submission

Worship While You Wait

"God Himself will provide the lamb for the burnt offering, my son." And the two of them went on together."

Genesis 22:8 ESV

As Abraham and Isaac journeyed up the mountain to worship God by offering a sacrifice, Isaac asked his father, Abraham, "Where is the lamb for the burnt offering?" It was a natural question. He could clearly see the wood, the fire, and the knife, but there was no lamb.

Abraham's response was a prophetic one, "God Himself will provide the lamb." Now Abraham could be this confident with his declaration because he knew God's promises to Him, and he had seen God's faithfulness time and time again. In Genesis 12:2, God promises Abram (who was later renamed Abraham) that he will be the father of many nations. Later (see Genesis 21), when Sarah asked Abraham to banish Hagar and Ishmael, God told him to do as Sarah requested but to be assured that nations would also come from Ishmael because he was Abraham's offspring (though not the promised child).

God's Word never fails and will not return to Him void. Abraham lived in a way that reflected a working knowledge of this truth. If nations were to come from Him through Isaac, then whatever the Lord intended through telling him to sacrifice his only son, whom he loved, could not go against God's promise to have nations come from Him.

So, as Abraham awaited the promise of nations, he continued to worship God faithfully. His journey to the mountaintop with Isaac was exactly that – worship. Making an animal sacrifice unto the Lord was a part of their worship then, and Abraham did not withhold his worship from the Lord. Though this instruction from God to sacrifice his son seemed to contradict the flourishing of the family line, Abraham moved in obedience anyway.

In Genesis 22:12, we see that an angel of the Lord cried out to Abraham to stop him from sacrificing Isaac. He goes on to say, *"Now I know that you fear God, because you have not withheld from Me your son, your only son"* (NIV). The fear referenced here is reverential fear, which points to honour and respect for who God is.

Journaling Prompt:
As you meditate on this, consider the questions below:

- Are your acts of worship today showing that you fear God?
- Is there anything that you are withholding from God as you go before Him?
- Are you walking and living confidently, knowing that God will not default on His promises to you?

Prayer Prompt:
Heavenly Father, I thank You that you are Jehovah-Jireh, the God who provides. Forgive me for not holding firmly to Your Word and not trusting You enough to worship wholeheartedly while I wait.

Today, Lord, I commit myself to You. Give me the faith of Abraham that I may go wherever You call me, keeping You front and centre, always. Help me to worship You through the trials and the pain, in Jesus's name I pray. Amen.

"I give thanks to you, O Lord my God, with my whole heart, and I will glorify your name forever."

Psalm 86:12 ESV

Let's Journal... Waiting on GOD:

From Sorrow to Submission

God's Timing is Perfect

*"But do not forget this one thing, dear friends: With the Lord a day is like a thousand years, and a thousand years are like a day. The Lord is not slow in keeping his promise, as some understand slowness.
Instead, He is patient with you, not wanting anyone to perish, but everyone to come to repentance."*

2 Peter 3:8-9 NIV

You may be tired of hearing this by now, but God's timing truly is perfect. His timing fits perfectly into His perfect will and plan for your life. The temptations will come often for you to push against God's timing for you, but today I want to remind you that the Lord is not slow in keeping His promise. Instead, He is patient with you, not wanting anyone to perish (see 2 Peter 3:8-9).

Is it possible that all this time you have been waiting on God, that He has been waiting on you too? Could He be waiting on you to see what He has already given you, what He has already placed in your hands? Could He be waiting on you to surrender this area of your life to Him so that His perfect will can be done in and through you? Could it be that God is waiting on you to repent of your impatience towards Him?

Think about Job who challenged God about his many afflictions. God's response of *"Where were you when I laid the earth's foundation?"* (see Job 38:4) reminds us of who He is as Creator. He has set the earth in its place, made boundaries for the seas and the clouds, and placed the stars in the sky. He created all, knows all, sees all, and that includes you in your waiting period.

Too often, we treat God as if He is simply there to give us the desires of our hearts, and we forget the condition attached to that promise. The Psalmist says,

> "**Delight yourself in the Lord**, and He will give you the desires of your heart. **Commit your way to the Lord**; trust in Him and He will…make your righteous reward shine like the dawn."
> Psalm 37:4-6 NIV, *emphasis mine*

By truly delighting in the Lord, your will aligns with His and His desires for you become the very things you desire for yourself.

Take hold of this: the thing that you have been waiting on for what feels like a thousand years, God can make happen in a day. Your job is to seek Him wholeheartedly, knowing and trusting that His plan for you is good and perfect. He wants to fulfil His plan for you that fits into the bigger picture that you may not be able to see. Will you trust Him enough to take the immediate next step He is showing you today?

Journal Prompt:
Reflect on your journey of waiting and write down any ways in which your actions, thoughts or words indicate that you have not trusted God's timing. Repent of this and then commit to honouring God's timing above your own.

Prayer Prompt:
Heavenly Father, Creator of the heavens and the earth, I thank You for considering me to be worthy of Your

attention, Your love, and Your grace. Forgive me for the times I have overstepped by becoming impatient with Your process, Lord. Help me to revere You and delight in You in the way I should. Help me to wait on Your timing for my life. I want to trust You completely. Please show me how. Meet me where I am that I may align with Your intention and timing for my life, in Jesus' name I pray. Amen.

"Wait for the Lord;
be strong, and let your heart take courage; wait for the Lord!"

Psalm 27:14 ESV

Let's Journal... Waiting on GOD:

From Sorrow to Submission

Wait on the Lord and be Renewed

"But those who wait for the Lord [who expect, look for, and hope in Him]
Will gain new strength and renew their power;
They will lift up their wings [and rise up close to God] like eagles [rising toward the sun];
They will run and not become weary, They will walk and not grow tired."

Isaiah 40:31 AMP

Waiting on God's promises can be a really challenging thing - waiting on someone you cannot see, believing for something that is to come but not knowing when, the questions in your mind can be endless. It can wear you down mentally and emotionally if you are not careful. With all the uncertainty though, there is one truth that stands above it all—God is faithful to His Word. He cannot lie.

As a couple, we have been waiting on the Lord for a child. We have been married for fourteen years and trying for eleven years to conceive. There have been many ups and downs emotionally, which we have learned over the years to process with the Lord. As we began to turn to Him instead of trying to deal with it on our own, He drew us closer to Himself and strengthened us through the sharing of our testimony. Now, we have learned to be expectant as we wait on God's promise, even when the doctors are saying it is impossible. He has truly strengthened and renewed us.

In Isaiah 40:31, we are assured that those who wait upon the Lord will be strengthened and renewed; they will draw closer to God, rising as eagles, and they will not become weary or faint.

But how is this possible? This kind of waiting is waiting with expectancy and confidence in God's Word. In this kind of waiting, you declare God's truth over your situation regardless of what the physical evidence says. This type of waiting means spending time with the Lord and moving according to His instructions and not according to your feelings. It requires you to let go of the time limits that you have in your mind within which God's promise must come to pass. Trust Him, trust His timing, and be obedient as you wait. He knows the plans He has for you (see Jeremiah 29:11).

Journaling Prompt:
How have you been waiting?

Ask God to examine your heart and reveal to you any area in which you have not been waiting well. Ask Him to show you how to align with His desire for you in this season.

Prayer Prompt:
Heavenly Father, I thank You that Your Word is true. I thank You that You provide refreshing and renewal to those who wait on You. As I continue on this journey, help me to be persistent in my pursuit of You, regardless of what is happening around me and how it feels. You are my strong tower and my source. I look to You today for renewal as I continue to wait on You, in Jesus' name I pray. Amen.

Let's Journal... Waiting on GOD:

From Sorrow to Submission

Bring Forth Fruit in its Season

*"Blessed is the man
Who walks not in the counsel of the
ungodly, Nor stands in the path of sinners,
Nor sits in the seat of the scornful;
But his delight is in the law of the Lord,
And in His law he meditates day and night.
He shall be like a tree Planted by the rivers of water,
That brings forth its fruit in its season,
Whose leaf also shall not wither;
And whatever he does shall prosper."*

Psalm 1:1-3 NIV

As you wait on the Lord, it can be very tempting to try to "help Him out." It may feel like He is being slow about fulfilling His promise or that time is running out for it to come to fruition. 2 Peter 3:9 assures us that God is not slow about fulfilling His promises. As we wait, the Lord continues to refine us, preparing us to receive the promise He has made to us.

Over the duration of our wait for children, the Lord has stripped and refined us in several areas. He has taught us the importance of putting Him first in everything that we do and learning to trust Him above all else. The desires He placed in our hearts were never meant to become idols. Our delight should always be in Him and His law.

When we take this approach, according to Psalm 1:2-3, we will be like a tree planted by the rivers of water, bringing forth fruit in its season. Don't miss this - it says, "in its season." There is a predestined time and place for the fulfilment of God's promise to you. He already has it written in His book. Your responsibility is to seek His will for you in your current season as He continues to faithfully prepare you for what is to come.

The verse goes on to say that the leaves will not wither, and whatever he does shall prosper. Although it may be tempting to dwell on what has not yet come to pass, there are mandates for you to fulfil right now. Will you allow your desire for what is to come prevent you from seeing the fruitfulness of your current season? It may not look how you expect it to, but you can be assured that whatever God is leading you to do now is ultimately for His glory and for good. He has promised you fruitfulness in whatever you do if you remain planted, rooted in Him, delighting in, and meditating on His law.

During this time of waiting for your promise, fruitfulness may look like:

- Pouring into the lives of others through volunteering, teaching, speaking, writing, etc.
- Improving your emotional health through intentional processing of traumas and pain.
- Building character through learning and growth opportunities. Making room to accommodate God's promise to you.

Journaling Prompt:
Spend some time with the Lord to learn what He is calling you to do in your current season as He prepares you for the next. What fruitfulness awaits you?

Prayer Prompt:
Dear Lord, please help me to recognize my current season and to embrace it fully. I want to delight in Your Word that

I may bring forth fruit in its season. Help me to rest in Your Sovereignty, in Jesus' name I pray. Amen.

"The Lord is not slow in keeping his promise, as some understand slowness. Instead he is patient with you, not wanting anyone to perish, but everyone to come to repentance."

2 Peter 3:9 ESV

Let's Journal ... Waiting on GOD:

From Sorrow to Submission

God is Still Faithful

"For when God made the promise to Abraham, He swore [an oath] by Himself, since He had no one greater by whom to swear, saying, "I will surely bless you and I will surely multiply you." And so, having patiently waited, he realized the promise [in the miraculous birth of Isaac, as a pledge of what was to come from God]."

Hebrews 6:13-15 AMP

Holding on to the promises of God can truly challenge us. We experience times of questioning and doubting what He had promised. We wonder if we heard or understood correctly or if we built up this expectation on our own. How can we really know that God said it and that we should hold on to it? That can be tough to answer, but the truest way to know is through your personal relationship with Him, knowledge of His Word, and true submission to His leadership. Nothing that God promises will go against His character or His Word as He is the same yesterday, today, and forever more. Once you have repented of your sins and accepted Jesus as Lord, the Holy Spirit resides within you (see Romans 8:3-4, 9-10). Your spirit comes alive, and you can hear from God. He speaks through His Word, through people, and directly to you in various ways. As you develop your relationship with God, you learn His voice and His character. He never changes.

In Hebrew 6:15, the author speaks of the result of Abraham waiting patiently on the promise of a son. Though the idea of waiting twenty-five years for the fulfilment of a promise may seem unfathomable (and surely not the preferred approach for many of us), never forget that GOD IS STILL FAITHFUL. He will not fall back on His promises. That is simply not in His character. Things may seem out of place, and the process may feel unpleasant, but GOD IS STILL FAITHFUL.

Remain fixed on Him, seeking His Kingdom first, fulfilling His purpose for you, knowing that as you continue to be about His business, He is about yours in ways you cannot even imagine.

Will you trust God to carry out His plan for your life?

Journaling Prompt:
The faithfulness of God never waivers. Even if it looks unlikely, He will keep His promises.

As you journal today, commit all your doubts, fears, and reservations to Him while committing to putting your faith entirely in Jesus Christ (which is an ongoing process).

Close out by noting three Scriptures that remind you that God is faithful to do what He said He will do.

Prayer Prompt:
Lord, please forgive me for any doubts, fears, or hesitations that I have been holding on to, those things that are preventing me from completely believing in You and Your promises for my life. Cleanse my heart and mind that I may wait patiently and expectantly for Your promises to be fulfilled as Abraham did. My life is Yours, Lord. Do with it as You will, in Jesus' name I pray. Amen.

"You, however, are not in the realm of the flesh but are in the realm of the Spirit, if indeed the Spirit of God lives in you."

Romans 8:9a NIV

Let's Journal... Waiting on GOD:

From Sorrow to Submission

Remain Confident in God

"Do not throw away your confidence; it will be richly rewarded. You need to persevere so that when you have done the will of God, you will receive what He has promised."

Hebrews 10:35 NIV

In Hebrews 10:32, the author calls back to memory your early days of salvation, when your enthusiasm for the Lord was high, and you were ready to follow Christ wholeheartedly. As you get down to verse 35, you see the author saying, "Do not throw away your confidence" (NIV). That same confidence you had in Christ earlier in your walk with Him is the same confidence you should maintain now, if not more, as you wait to see the promise come to pass. This confidence is placed squarely in God, not in self. It is a product of your faith in Him.

You can be assured that when God promises something, He will do it.

Take a moment to think about Abraham who had Ishmael outside of God's promise, and yet, God chose to still bring forth twelve tribes from Ishmael (see Genesis 17:20 and Genesis 25:12-18). Recall that one of God's promises to Abraham was that he would be the father of a multitude of nations. So, though Ishmael was not the promised child, he was still Abraham's child, and God honoured His promise to Abraham through Isaac, as well as Ishmael. God said it; therefore, He will do it. You can remain confident of that even when it looks like things are not going as you think they should.

And even if you have made some mistakes along the way, God stands ready to forgive you and continue walking with you toward the promise once you genuinely repent of your sins. I encourage you today not to allow the enemy any room in your mind to convince you that you have forfeited your promise. God's Word stands firm and will not return to Him void. If your actions, or inactions, are delaying the fulfilment of the promise, then it is your role to seek God for guidance on how to move forward. Go before Him honestly and vulnerable; let Him search your heart and reveal to you where the issue lies. Then, you repent where needed and commit to walking in alignment with God moving forward.

Abraham was forgiven and the promises fulfilled to him and his bloodline. Why? Because he submitted himself to God completely. By the time he was tested regarding the sacrifice of Isaac, Abraham was so confident in God that he moved into action without complaint. He knew that what God had promised would come to fruition.

Verse 35 of Hebrews 10 goes on to say that this confidence will be **richly rewarded**. Your confidence in God is reflected in your responses to Him and His instructions. This does not go unnoticed by God. Your promises await you.

Journaling Prompt:
As you journal today, ask God to:

- Remind you of His promise(s) to you.
- Show you any actions, thoughts, or speech that you need to repent of.
- Renew your confidence in Him.

Prayer Prompt:
Heavenly Father, I surrender all to You. Show me my heart and any areas in which I may have lost my confidence in You. I repent of this, Father, and I commit today to aligning with Your truth and Your promises for my life. Renew my confidence in You, Lord. Help me to walk out my faith daily, even during this wait, in the way that truly glorifies You, in Jesus' name I pray. Amen.

"Remember those earlier days after you had received the light, when you endured in a great conflict full of suffering."

Hebrews 10:32 NIV

Let's Journal... Waiting on GOD:

From Sorrow to Submission

Make Room for Your Promise

"And if their hearts were still remembering what they left behind, they would have found an opportunity to go back. But they couldn't turn back for their hearts were fixed on what was far greater, that is, the heavenly realm!"

Hebrews 11:15-16 TPT

At this point of your journey, you may be certain of God's promise to you. You may be praying consistently and fervently for it to come to pass, but are you making room for it? Are you preparing physically, mentally, emotionally, financially, and spiritually to receive what you have been praying for?

In Hebrews 11, we are shown that if our sights are set on what has already gone, then we will always find a reason to go back - returning to what felt easier to bear. It feels easier to remain in your current state and not persevere in prayer for the promise. It feels easier to let someone else do it. But if you are committed to doing the will of God, then it will require pressing beyond your comfort zone and remaining fixed on what is far greater.

Waiting is generally challenging for us as human beings, and we can be easily tempted to take shortcuts or to remain in what is comfortable. But, today, I want you to know that God is doing a new thing, and it is time for you to:

*"Forget the former things; do not dwell on the past.
See, I am doing a new thing!
Now it springs up; do you not perceive it?
I am making a way in the wilderness and streams in the wasteland."*
Isaiah 43:18-19 NIV

The "new thing" for you may look like a renewed perspective, healed emotions, a rejuvenated marriage, spiritual growth...and the list goes on. Make yourself available to God and allow Him to do His perfect work in you. When He makes that way in the wilderness, will you walk in it?

There is no turning back to what was. Set your eyes and heart on what is ahead, that which you have been promised. Pray for it, but also actively prepare for it. What is ahead is far greater than what has gone. No, your "best days" are not behind you, they are ahead of you in the heavenly realm. What you choose to do today, how you choose to respond today, matters.

Journaling Prompt:
As you sit with the Lord today, ask Him if there is any area in which you have been focusing on the things of the past instead of what is ahead. Take note of His response and follow His instructions.

Prayer Prompt:
Lord, I thank You that I can trust in Your plan, which is far greater than anything I can think or imagine. Please forgive me for holding on to the past instead of preparing for the future You have for me.

Help me to focus on what is ahead and to truly place my

faith and hope in You alone. Show me the areas in which You want me to make room for Your promise. I submit myself to Your perfect will today as I say, "Have Your way, Lord." In Jesus' name I pray. Amen.

"Now this I know:
The Lord gives victory to His anointed. He answers him from His heavenly sanctuary with the victorious power of His right hand."

Psalm 20:6 NIV

Let's Journal ••• Waiting on GOD:

From Sorrow to Submission

Say Goodbye to Doubt

"But as for me, I will look to the Lord; I will wait for the God of my salvation; my God will hear me."

Micah 7:7 ESV

When everything around you seems to be going against the thing you are waiting for, are you still standing firm on God's Word? Are you convinced of God's faithfulness?

There came a point in our journey where we had to choose between the thing that many around us were saying we should do and what we knew God had told us to do. Taking the decision to go God's way came with some questions, some ridicule, and some challenging days of wondering if we made the right choice. But, ultimately, knowing that God told us to wait on His solution was greater than anything else anyone could have said. Even now, as we continue to wait, we look to the Lord, trusting that He hears us.

Doubt breeds confusion. When you allow doubt in, you begin to wonder and waver. You become double-minded, and this is an opportunity for the enemy to get a foothold in your mind, taking your focus away from the truth and the promises of God.

I am encouraging you today to look to God, wait for Him, knowing that He hears you. Stand firm on His Word, cast aside all doubt and fear, knowing that God is faithful. Is this always easy? Absolutely not! But it is possible, especially when your hope remains anchored in the Lord, and you have a strong, godly community supporting you.

Sometimes, God sends His help, love, and encouragement through people. Let them in. This point may seem unrelated, but think about it: what is your reason for holding your desires so close to your chest and refusing to share them with anyone? Are you doubting that they will understand or maybe doubting that they will even care? Are you believing that all "people" are unkind and only want to hear what you are going through to gossip about it?

These are all doubts. You may have been hurt by people before. You may even still be healing from some of that pain. But that does not mean that everyone is bad. Seek discernment and wisdom from the Lord to identify the people He wants you to commune with. God wants you to have fruitful relationships with others. Trust Him to guide you in this area as well.

Journaling Prompt:
Take a moment to reflect on what beliefs you have been holding on to regarding other people.

Are you isolating yourself because you doubt that someone else will care for you? Are you ready to submit this area of your life completely to God, trusting that He will help you to navigate relationships and increase your discernment so you share appropriately as you grow?

Prayer Prompt:
Lord, please forgive me for doubting You. Forgive me for doubting Your deep care for me and Your faithfulness to the promise You have spoken to me. It is ultimately all for

Your glory, Lord. Please help me to remember that so I will take a position of submission to You in all things.

I will look to You, Lord. I will wait on You, trusting that You hear me. You are faithful and just to complete the work You have started in me. I stand on Your Word today, placing my hope entirely in You, in Jesus' name. Amen.

"If any of you lacks wisdom, you should ask God, who gives generously to all without finding fault, and it will be given to you."

James 1:5 NIV

Let's Journal ... Waiting on GOD:

From Sorrow to Submission

Hold Firm to God's Promises

"But he [Abraham] did not doubt or waver in unbelief concerning the promise of God, but he grew strong and empowered by faith, giving glory to God, being fully convinced that God had the power to do what He had promised. Therefore, his faith WAS CREDITED TO HIM AS RIGHTEOUSNESS (right standing with God)."

Romans 4:20-22 AMP

There is a reason Abraham is hailed as "The Father of Faith." Against all hope, he was confident that he would see the promise of God in the form of a child being born to him and Sarah. He was faithful and unwavering. The further he went on his journey with the Lord, the more empowered he became by faith. He was fully convinced that God would do exactly what He said He would do.

His faith was exhibited through his continued obedience to the instructions of God. This same faith was attributed to him as righteousness. Does it mean that Abraham never made a mistake? By no means. But what it does mean is that those mistakes were covered by God's grace. Abraham was given the chance to repent of his wrongdoings and to continue his journey with God, and that's what he did each time. He chose God's way. Again, this was a strong display of his faith and belief in God.

It was his confidence in God that allowed him to pass the test of sacrificing Isaac. Genesis 22:12 says: *"for now I know that you fear and revere God, since you have not held back from Me or begrudged giving Me your son, your only son."* (AMPC).

Abraham displayed no resentment towards God for this request. How is that possible? By complete faith in God. This displays a significant level of trust in who God is and what He has said.

Abraham was even further empowered because he was very clear on what the promise was. So, he knew what he was holding on to, regardless of how the circumstances looked. As he ascended that mountain with his son whom he was asked to sacrifice unto God, he was bold enough to declare that the Lord would provide a lamb for the sacrifice because he knew that Isaac was the promised son through whom many nations would be birthed. Therefore, God would make a way. His hope was in God's adherence to His promise, nothing else. Abraham was not concerned about a plan B. He was doing as God asked and trusting God with the rest. Are you?

Journaling Prompt:
As you meditate on this, consider the questions below for your journaling:

- Are you confident of God's specific promise(s) to you? What are they? (Include Scriptural support for each promise as well).
- Are you holding firm to His promise(s)?
- Is your faith being displayed through obedience even when it seemingly doesn't make sense?
- Is there anything that God has instructed you to do that you are holding back or feeling resentful about?

Prayer Prompt:
Abba, Father, I glorify Your name because You alone are worthy to be praised. Forgive me for holding back from You. Increase my faith that I may release the resentment, the hurt, the pain and instead, hold tight to your faithful promises. Renew my mind, Lord, that I may see Your faithfulness. Help me to choose swift obedience without contempt, knowing that You give only good gifts to Your children so I can trust You with all of me. Help me to keep Your Word always hidden in my heart, in Jesus's name I pray. Amen.

"In Him we were also chosen, having been predestined according to the plan of Him who works out everything in conformity with the purpose of His will..."

Ephesians 1:11 NIV

Let's Journal... Waiting on GOD:

From Sorrow to Submission

Wait Well

"I have been crucified with Christ and I no longer live, but Christ lives in me. The life I now live in the body, I live by faith in the Son of God, who loved me and gave Himself for me."

Galatians 2:20 NIV

A place of complete surrender is one in which you remember that your life is not your own. You were bought with a price – the blood of Jesus Christ, who died for you. What greater price is there? He gave His all for you so that you can choose to live your life for Him, drawing others unto Him.

In Galatians 2:20, when Paul speaks about Christ living in him and living by faith in the Son of God, he is acknowledging that Jesus Christ is Lord of his life. This is where Paul identifies that his decisions are governed by Christ. It is a humbling place to be and should surely resonate as a goal for us all.

As the Lord brings healing, clarity, freedom, and restored hope to your life, His desire is for you to see yourself as He sees you. You are His masterpiece (see Ephesians 2:10) who has a perfect purpose as a part of His master plan. He loves you immensely, and He knows the plans He has for you (see Jeremiah 29:11). Understand too that He also has a plan for the others impacted by your journey.

Your wait is not about punishment or failure. It is about God's perfect plan and how your story fits into that. He wants you to do it His way because there is so much more that is impacted by your obedience, surrender, and submission than you can ever see. After all, the earth is the Lord's and the fullness thereof (see Psalm 24:1), and with that, He works all things together for the good of those who love Him and are called according to His purpose (see Romans 8:28).

Consider Hannah, who waited and prayed for a child while enduring the ridicule of Peninah. Yet, Samuel was born right in time to become the prophet of the land when they needed him.

Consider David, who waited years to be crowned as king, all while enduring persecution and trials that seemed endless. Yet, at the time he ascended to king was exactly when he needed to be there. This same David was anointed as king by Samuel for whom Hannah prayed.

When you feel tempted to believe that there is something wrong with you because the promise has not yet come to pass, remember that God's thoughts are higher, His ways are higher, and He is the One with the master plan.

Today, I encourage you to wait well for the timing of the Lord. Seek to live a life fully surrendered to Him and His ways so that you, like Paul, can live your life by faith in the Son of God. After all, it is all about Him.

> *"All things were made through Him, and without Him was not anything made that was made."* - John 1:3 ESV

Journaling Prompt:
Ask God to show you how you have been waiting. If you have not been leaning into His Sovereignty, ask for His forgiveness and for His direction on how to wait well.

Some things to consider may include:

- How have you been waiting?
- Has the thing you are waiting for taken the place of God in your life?
- Has it become an idol?

Do you find yourself complaining about what you don't yet have, rather than being grateful for what you do have?

Take some time today to reflect on how you have been waiting. Write it down and repent where necessary.

Prayer Prompt:
Jesus, You are Lord of my life. Forgive me for taking that for granted and treating my life as if it is only for me. You have given everything for me. I want to live for You alone. Please help me to crucify my flesh daily so that You can shine through me, even while I wait. I want to wait well, Lord. I want to reflect You, even through the trials, and remain faithful and steadfast, knowing that my entire existence is because of You and, ultimately, it is for You. Have Your way in me, Lord. I surrender myself to You today, Jesus. Amen.

"I praise you, for I am fearfully and wonderfully made. Wonderful are your works; my soul knows it very well." - Psalm 139:14 ESV

Let's Journal ... Waiting on GOD:

From Sorrow to Submission

www.ingramcontent.com/pod-product-compliance
Lightning Source LLC
Chambersburg PA
CBHW060848050426
42453CB00008B/892